BOLD. BEAUTIFUL. BRILLIANT.

Bold. Beautiful. Brilliant.
Copyright 2012 by Aubrey Rinehart.

Requests for information should be addressed to:
Aubrey Rinehart PO Box 60331, Palo Alto, CA 94306

Rinehart, Aubrey
Bold. Beautiful. Brilliant. : Supermodel Secrets for Every Woman / Aubrey Rinehart p. cm.
ISBN 978-0-9859638-2-8 (softcover)

Printed in the United States of America.

A SPECIAL THANK YOU TO THE CONTRIBUTING PHOTOGRAPHERS (in order of appearance): Robert Trama Photography (cover), Rummy Makmar Photography, Stuart Locklear Photographer, Kanoa Utler Photography, Frank Lee Photography, Timothy Engle Photography and Robert Trama Photography.

By: Aubrey Rinehart

TO BECKY BUGGER, HER DAUGHTER KAMRYNN BUGGER

& THE WOMEN OF A NEW GENERATION.

BOLD. BEAUTIFUL. BRILLIANT.

SUPERMODEL SECRETS FOR EVERY WOMAN

CONTENTS

"*Whatever you want in life, other people are going to want it too. Believe in your-self enough to accept the idea that you have an equal right to it.*"   DIANE SAWYER

INTRODUCTION

I GET MEASURED ON MONDAY AND I WEAR A SIZE ZERO. At Friday's fitting I'm busting out of a four. On Sunday, the zero is way too big for me and they have to make alterations before the runway show. So what size am I and where do I fit in? When a potential client asks me what size I am, which one should I answer? Do you think that they will like me more if I'm a zero or are they looking for a four? Is there one defining quality that will make me perfect in their eyes? In my own eyes, I'm perfectly perfect on Monday, Friday and Sunday, and what they think has just become part of my job, not part of who I am. Claudia Schiffer said, "*The difference between the girls today and models of the past is that we are not only interested in fashion: we are going in so many different directions at once. We work harder — at night and on weekends.*" Being a Bold, Beautiful and Brilliant example of you is up to you; no matter your profession! You have to take charge of who you are, regardless of what anyone else says that you are, and doing so is a full time job. (In addition to whatever other random jobs you are doing to pay the bills. If you want this, it's going to be a load of work.)

Being Bold, Beautiful and Brilliant isn't about the beauty that everyone sees in you. It's about the beauty that we find inside ourselves and turning that positive energy into a machine that can ultimately conquer all of the negativity that presents itself to us on a daily basis. The confidence that can be found inside of all of us is something that is more beautiful than we could ever show physically, but taking care of our bodies, respecting ourselves, and adding a little polish is the icing on the cupcake of confidence.

Being Bold is made up of lots of different things. Developing a thick skin is definitely the first project on your to do list of supermodel secrets. This is something that you need to have in everyday life, not just at casting calls. Everyone that you meet is going to have an opinion of you, whether it's an agent or a neighbor. Being Bold isn't just about being a super-model, it's about developing your super-you.

In order to find that diva that lies in wait on the inside you will have to develop a confidence and self-respect that seeps from your pores. You are going to have to learn to be poised in every situation, even the most uncomfortable ones. Who knows what kind of crazy stuff you are going to come across, and being poised is not always going to be easy. I've had my share of hard situations. When the old lady with six cats and a six pack a day habit in 12B tells you that you need to eat a cheeseburger, you will eventually learn to smile and wave instead of your gut reaction to go buy that burger and throw it at her.

Figure out exactly where you want to be in your life and your career and stay motivated to be there. Sit down and define yourself, commit to being the best super-you that you can possibly be, and don't stray. It's not going to be easy and you will probably get slapped in the face a time or two, but you can do this. You are the one that matters and whoever decides otherwise isn't worth the worry.

Part of staying motivated includes creating your own opportunities. I'm sorry, but you cannot count on having the *"Giselle Bundchen"* experience where some magical modeling fairy swoops down while you are chillin' at the mall with a nonfat mocha and thrust into overnight supermodel stardom. Create opportunities, audition when you don't think that you have a chance, and then push yourself out past your comfort zone until you think you've done all you can do, and then push harder.

Being mentally prepared at every casting call, every time you wake up, is so important to the aftermath of any situation that you might be put in to. You never know if the judge at the casting call woke up to a cold shower or a crappy cup of coffee. You have no control over what they are going to think about you. You are, however, in control of what you think of you, and finding a great group of friends who understand what you are going through is going to be vital in staying positive on a daily basis. You can't do this alone, but be sure that your support group is a positive one, and stay away from negative idiots that try to suck you into their sadomasochistic world of blue-grey nothingness.

We'll move on to being Beautiful. Beauty is only skin deep but taking care of your whole being is the most beautiful person you can be. I've got lots of easy tricks about being healthy. Because really, that is what it's all about. There is no miracle diet for those of you who want to lose weight, and no surgery that will magically make you have a beautiful soul. If you eat right, exercise, and carefully pick and choose your extra-curricular activities, you will find that you feel better physically, which makes you stronger mentally, and ultimately produces the most beautiful person on the outside that you could possibly imagine. You may look into the mirror and see someone who doesn't fit the idea of what beautiful is defined as by society, but you will know on the inside that you are exactly what you were intended to be. Don't try and transform your body into the stereotypical frame, try and transform your heart and soul into realizing how extraordinary that you are just the way you are. Once you accept yourself and learn to take care of your body and yourself, you will be on the fast track to experiencing joys in this world that you didn't even know existed.

So once you purchase a shiny new car, it's absolutely perfect, just what you wanted, it doesn't stay that way on its own, right? You have to maintain it, develop it, add extras, "soop it up". That's where Brilliant comes in. Don't ever be satisfied with being satisfied! Always set goals and strive for new opportunities. Further your education. Learn new things, even if they have nothing to do with your goals. Do things just because you want to. My mother was in her 50's before she finally decided to take an art class that she wanted to take her entire life, but she'd just never had enough time. Make time. Something that I always say is "you only have one chance to live today." Isn't that so simple, really?

One chance.

It doesn't matter what religion you are, what you believe in, where you believe you are going. That statement applies to everyone. You only get one chance. Today will never, ever come again and it should be embraced. I'm not saying that you need to go out and do all this crazy stuff every single day, I'm just saying that your life will be so much more fulfilling if you wake up every morning remembering, "Hey! This is the only time I get to wake up today." Walk with footsteps that are excited to be blessed with every opportunity that you may come across today, and do so knowing that you are a brilliant piece of artwork, no matter what size, color or shape that you may be. There is no possibility of a reproduction of you. Remember that in addition to all of the hustle and bustle that life presents you with, your body was built with the need to relax, calm down and breathe. A Beautiful, healthy you, is a relaxed, stress-free you.

You might wonder how I know this or what right do I have to tell you how to act or be. I have been there, I am still there. Inside every beautiful woman is an insecure little girl who has always been told that she is too skinny or too fat, not smart enough or too much of a nerd. Everyone loves to judge, and in the modeling world, it comes with the territory. When I was twelve years old, I sprouted up 7 inches in 7 months! By the time that I settled in at a short 5'11, I had gained inches in height but not a pound in weight. I was still weighing in at the same 90 pounds that I was in July when I started to shoot up. I resorted to baggy clothes and flats but I still got made fun of. Looks of disgust and judgment came from all sorts of people who had no idea what they were talking about and I earned all kinds of great nicknames like "Twig" and "Beanpole."

Growing up I never really knew where I fit in, I didn't look Asian enough to be Chinese and I wasn't European enough to be white. Defining who I was as a teenager, in a world full of stereotypes was incredibly difficult for me. When I turned sixteen, I finally broke the 100 pound mark, but I was still taller and skinner than everyone else. Talk about self-conscious. So here I am, this sixteen year old girl who is addicted to cute shoes and loves fashion, and adding a three inch heel to my already towering 5'11 frame was bringing even more attention to the fact that I soared over all of my friends. Strangers and friends would say things like:

> "You are too skinny, seriously eat more."
> "You need to put on a pound or two."

Do people randomly walk up to overweight or obese people and say "Holy crap, you are so fat! You need to lose some weight." No, people don't do that because it's disrespectful. In my opinion, telling a skinny girl, whose story you do not know, to put on a pound or two is exactly the same thing. I had no control over my weight or height at the time. I ate when I was hungry and that was it. I am now extremely healthy. I take care of my body and I don't abuse it with foods that are bad for me. I don't eat fast food or drink copious amounts of alcohol. I stay away from soda, not because I'm afraid of gaining weight, but because it's simply not good for me. I've actually been denied medical coverage, denied coverage, for being too thin. Seriously? The insurance company said that I weigh "Fifteen pounds less than" what I should weigh for being 5'11. Have you ever heard of someone being denied coverage for "Eating too much McDonalds?" NO. And now I hear radio commercials to "check with your ppo provider for medical coverage for weight loss programs." It is absolutely ridiculous what this world puts us through when it comes to our appearance. What am I supposed to do about that? Eat crappy food and stop exercising so that I really do get sick and need medical attention? I was afraid to try and break into the modeling world because I did not want to be ridiculed even more. I knew that there would be more teasing, more names, more denial, more awkward, self-conscious moments with a stranger.

What happened? Why did I decide that being Bold, Beautiful & Brilliant was my only option? It was because the only other option I had was to be dull, dreary and depressing. I was in love and engaged. All of my dreams were coming true. I had a great job and life was amazing. Then life got real. It was December. Beautiful, white magic floated through the air and everyone I saw looked so happy. Alive. But the air was being sucked out of my life and I was slowly suffocating. Suddenly I was going through a ridiculously messy break up, full of all of the angst you could possibly imagine. My job was becoming more and more stressful with mounting hours topped by being assaulted by my supervisor. Now I was not only being judged by my looks, but I was also the hot topic of choice in the "nasty rumor" section at work. Human resources were useless and I was left alone, with no one but my sweet cat, which became very sick and had to be put down.

I had no one left to talk to about it except my family. Just when I thought life was teaching me a lesson on tough times, life showed me how tough it could really get. The phone call that turned things from awful to horrific still rings in my ears, but the sound has turned from deafening to awakening. My stepdad had unexpectedly passed away.

Obscurity.

Depression overwhelmed my soul. I stopped eating, not to look better or lose weight, but because there was no purpose in eating. There was no purpose in waking. Purpose was driven by bodily functions that forced me to move, like breathing. I dropped ten pounds and began to wither away into a world of emptiness and hopelessness. One bright February morning, trying to hope and will my luck to chance, I received news that a friend that I had known since junior high, had somehow lost sight of the beautiful things in life like I had. Only for this friend it was too late. This person had overdosed, and their only chance to crawl out of the depths was now impossible. Even today, I have very little recollection of that January, February and March. A wave of something ethereal came over me and before I knew it I decided that I was no longer going to slowly cease to exist. I didn't have any emotions left to be crushed and I couldn't be hurt any worse. My glass was already overflowing, what was another droplet going to hurt? So I gathered up every bit of drive that was left inside of me and I jumped into the modeling world. I went for it. And I was ridiculed. I was picked apart and still denied. But I was stronger. Bolder. It didn't matter anymore. I had discovered a secret that I never knew before.

I've come to realize that even if you are a person who has lost a parent like I have, your job as their child is not over. Somewhere, somehow, they are still watching over you, and it is your job to continue to make them proud. It gets easier the second you realize that no depression, fame, or acceptance is going to replace them. Nothing that anyone can say or do or pick at will ever be able to take away who I am in my soul. In the darkest, deepest part of my body, the part that no one can make fun of or pick at, lies the most bold, beautiful, brilliant person that you could ever imagine. It's up to me to make them see that, and if they don't, then that is their loss. That is why I am writing this book to you. I want to help every teenage girl, women young and old, to find that amazing part of them that is impermeable to the destruction that this world throws at them.

Whether you are a struggling model trying to figure out how to make it all work, a young woman who just wants to be a better you, or a teenage girl who isn't sure if she has what it takes to be what she wants to be, whether that is a model, actress, executive, or chef, being Bold, Beautiful and Brilliant from the inside out will help you in every aspect of your life. This isn't a book to teach you how to become that super-you, there will be lots of tips along the way for those of you who are thinking about entering that world of fashion. This isn't a book that is going to transform your outer beauty and tell you how much weight you need to lose or what size you should be. This is a book that is going to help you reach down in to your soul and pull out the most magnificent, spectacular inner beauty that you have and teach you how to show it to the world. Because it is there. It's up to you to find it.

"Be bold. If you're going to make an error, make a doozy, and don't be afraid to hit the ball." *BILLIE JEAN KING*

CHAPTER ONE | BOLD

"A THICK SKIN IS A GIFT FROM GOD." -*KONRAD ADENAUER.* Let's start out talking about that thick skin that you need to start growing right about, let's see, Now! Going out knowing that you have what it takes but understanding that others don't always recognize your awesomeness is something that will prove to be so vital to you. Developing a thick skin in the modeling industry is something that is necessary, but I find that it is definitely something that will help you in every aspect of your life. But be wise enough to understand that developing a thick skin is different than losing sight of that sensitive part of your personality. Keep her too. Someone recently said to me – "your appearance is your first opportunity to be rejected." People are instant critics. Everyone that you meet, whether it's an agent or your grandma, is going to have advice for you. Take most of it with a grain of salt.

I've been told so many things about what I need to change about myself. I've heard it ALL—too big, too small; too tall, too short; too *"hippie"*; not enough Asian, not enough white; boobs too big, boobs too small. There is absolutely no way that I can be everything that everyone wants me to be. It's just not possible. It's hard not to let all that criticism get you down. It's challenging not to get discouraged. At first, I didn't understand why I'd get called to so many auditions and not get the part. But I've realized that every time I go to an audition; it's also a networking opportunity. I have the chance to stand in front of new casting directors and producers. It's the same as going to job interviews. Know what your skills are and try to show them in the best light. Someone who is mean to you may just be having a bad day, or a bad life, but that's not your problem. Remember to be completely and selflessly self-involved with you. The only opinion that matters is your own!

Learn to understand that all sorts of factors are going on behind the scenes. When it comes to go-see's and auditions, most casting agents already have an idea of what they are looking for long before you walk in the door. They can take one look at you, think that you are absolutely gorgeous, and know right away that you are absolutely NOT perfect for the part or the shoot. There is always something that you don't know. I was once cast for a runway gig for an Indonesian designer. The casting director booked everyone from an open call except me. I was out of town and she booked me from my pictures. During the process, she had to have asked a thousand times if my hair was still exactly the same as the photos that were submitted. Over and over I assured her they were but was quite confused by her obsession with my hair. On the day of the event, I was designated to a different hair and makeup artist than the other girls. Not questioning, as my job is on the runway not behind the scenes, I finally realized what her obsession was about. The designer had not only made some very gorgeous garments, but had also designed a very elaborate hairpiece from jet-black extensions. If I'd shown up to the same casting blonde, brunette or redheaded, I would not have been cast for the same part by the same casting director because they were looking for something else. Other girls at that show were upset that they didn't get the same elaborate treatment. But the client wanted one thing – a 5'11" size 2 runway model with jet-black hair. I just happened to fit that part. But during the entire casting process, I didn't have a clue.

There is just no way that you are going to be able to please everyone and you are constantly going to be put into situations where you just can't make everyone happy. During my career as a model, I have a designer that I have gone out of my way for and developed what I thought was a really close relationship with. I was there for her when she needed me and I did what it took to stand out to her as a model and employee. Soon a time came that she was putting an editorial together, and I was so stoked. After I waited a while and finally got up the guts to find out if I'd be a part of it, she said that the production team had chosen other models. Of course my heart was broken, of course I was disappointed and of course I was angry. However, I sat back, thought about it, and reminded myself that there had to be factors in this situation that I couldn't see. I reminded myself that everything happens for a reason, and that this just wasn't the right opportunity for me. I made sure that the designer knew that I understood and that I hoped that we could work together again on another project sometime. I kept my integrity and in that moment, I'm sure that I left more of a lasting impression than the one that I had worked so hard to build up in the months before. She would remember me, not because of all the things I did for her, but because of the way I behaved when she couldn't do something for me. Another huge part of being bold is taking advice from the ladies of yesteryear.

POISED: {poi·zd}
adjective
I. Assured; Composed
II. Held balanced or steady in readiness

Audrey Hepburn was the picture of a poised woman. Her solemn facial expressions and hard to read body language left her as an icon of refinement, loveliness, and beauty. She once said, *"For beautiful eyes, look for the good in others; for beautiful lips, speak only words of kindness; and for poise, walk with the knowledge that you are never alone."* Basically this is the most amazing thing that you can do for yourself. When you find good things, even in people who don't deserve it, you begin to glow. You start to present yourself with this aura of class and dignity. I recently produced 2 complete episodes of my new talk show. It was very stressful and required many, many details. The night before filming was to take place, the director called me to tell me that the location he'd assured me would work months ago was not going to work. It was 9 PM the night before and I'd asked my entire team to be there at noon the next day. I had a matter of hours to scrounge up a new location. I was furious! And it took every ounce of strength in me not to really speak my mind. Plus, I had to focus on the task at hand. For a fleeting second, I wanted to throw in the towel on the whole ordeal. I knew I had to hang up the phone for fear of a long line of expletives escaping. So I bit my tongue, hung up and racked my brain. Were it not for the support of my true and valued friends, I think I might have lost my mind. I was able to lean on them for support and when necessary a huge favor – to which I converted a friend's living room into a temporary studio and made due. There is no amount of outer beauty that can surpass the hypnotizing beauty of a woman who shimmers from the inside out.

Being a poised, classy woman is a thing of the past. In today's world there is an excess amount of raunchiness and disregard for the way that we treat our bodies and in many sectors, the partying, *"I'm gonna do what I want because I can"* attitude is embraced and celebrated. This might work for some people for about ten seconds. When the fad fades, those women are back to trying to figure out exactly who they are again. Women demand respect and accountability, but if you aren't presenting yourself with that same air, I doubt you will get it.

Remembering to stay motivated is such a big deal. There will be days when it totally sucks to wake up. There are going to be times that you feel like this world has slapped you in the face one too many times. Nobody ever said it was going to be easy. If this is really where you want to be, you need to sit back and remember why. Remember the drive that you first felt when you started your journey. Sit down and literally write down the reasons that you are doing this, remember what you love about where you are headed and what you want to be. Set high goals for yourself and set low goals. Accomplish the small things first and take it day by day until you start reaching milestone after milestone. Celebrate the little accomplishments and be proud when small blessings happen in your life.

I mentioned earlier that having a strong support group is vital to your survival in the modeling industry, but it is also vital to anyone in any industry. You have to learn to trust people, to rely on people. Take your time and choose your friends wisely, find likeminded people who have the same morals and values as you do. Just like I'm sure your mother told you once, you are who you hang out with. Be sure that you associate with positive people who want to build you up and not bring you down. That doesn't necessarily mean that they tell you every single day how wonderful you are, but negativity breeds negativity. If your support system consists of a bunch of Debbie downers, it is not good for you.

I was in a relationship that turned south fast and I needed to get out immediately. We were living together and he said he needed space; move out. That effectively made me homeless. Away from family, I didn't really have anywhere to turn. Were it not for one of my friends who I've known since high school, I don't know what I would have done. He took me in, supported what I needed to heal and brought new light to my life. I feared ridiculous things like being berated for leaving a cup out since that's what had been happening. But my friend assured me that wasn't right and not how things would be. He was there when all I wanted to do was cry. He was there to make me laugh. And he was there just to be there. Having a good group of friends *(real friends, not Facebook friends)* is an important building block in being mentally prepared before you head out to feed the vultures.

Be a realist. Don't head out expecting to knock the socks off of everyone that you meet. Stay confident and remain true to who you are, no matter what challenges you are presented with or what opportunities may arise that could cause you to question your morals, values or compromising who you are motivated to be. I've seen girls who were clearly uncomfortable in the ultra-revealing outfits that designers put them in but for fear of upsetting her agent, the designer, the show producer or lord knows who else, she said nothing. Did I mention she was 14? The top completely exposed her breast and she was going to have to walk out to a crowd of hundreds. I leaned over to her and said "You can say no." She looked at me in shock and said "But I don't want him to call my agent." After quite a bit of reassurance and guiding, she resented to expressing her concerns and he put her in a different outfit—no problems caused. The designer was a bit of a pompous prick but it saddens me how fearfully she remained quiet. What's sadder is her mother was in the building as parental consent and she didn't confide in her mother either. No gig or amount of money is worth surrendering your inner you. There is no way that you can predict what the people you are about to face are looking for, so remembering that this is not about your idea of your beauty, it is about the idea that was already formed in their head before you walked in the door. It's pretty ridiculous, really. A predefined idea of what you are supposed to be? How is that even fair? You would think that they would post things like, "Only all-the-way Asian girls need apply," or "Must weigh exactly 105.79932 and ½ pounds to be considered for this shoot." But no, it is almost like "the man" thrives on our misery. "Everyone please come out and audition so that we can crush the dreams of 99% of the people who walk through the door." This is where we are learning to change. They don't have the power to crush your dreams. Don't give them the power. The power of what happens to your dreams is yours. Your dream job does not exist. You must create it.

Once you are mentally prepared and you've got your insecurities under control, start to look at each encounter differently. Remind yourself that each audition, each meeting, each cup of coffee is an opportunity that is screaming for your attention. Never look back and say, "I should have talked to that person, I should have sold myself more." It is going to be really hard for you to stay positive and not get frustrated with the denial. A lot of girls get called to casting after casting and still come home empty handed. Don't take this as an insult, take it as a compliment. Your agent sees something in you if he or she is placing you at casting after casting. There is something that they are inspired by, and you just have to patiently wait for someone else to see that too. Sometimes your castings will get cancelled or you will get turned away at the door. Your agent has no control over this, and in this business, they are just as disappointed that you didn't get the job as you are. You have to keep yourself from getting frustrated about things that you have no control over, not only at castings, but in your everyday life. You can't control that it rains on the one day that you have time to go to the park. You cannot control the fact that the last guy you went on a date with had more cats than your grandma. You can't control the fact that the casting agent had one too many long island iced teas the night before. Crappy things will happen, I guarantee it. It is the attitude that you have towards those crappy things that will define what opportunities you grasp. Yes, there are charmed people in this world that seemingly have everything fall into their laps, like little raindrops of opportunity that just continuously shower them. But most normal, non-fairy tale folks like you and me, have to work their butts off to get what they want. It might take you years to find that pivotal role that catapults you into supermodel stardom.

One of the hardest things about being rejected is not getting any feedback. But really, it is so simple. You are a brunette and they wanted a blonde, they wanted someone shorter or were looking for someone more masculine. Most of all, you have to focus your energy into believing that it just wasn't meant to be. As long as you went into that casting with a positive mental attitude, you were prepared, polite and punctual, and you gave 100%, practicing every moment and being ready to work every second, then you cannot walk away with any angst over not getting the job. There was just someone who was a better fit. It's really that simple. It is not because you are horrid and you should have never ever thought that you could do this. It is not because you smelled funny. It just wasn't your time. Your time will come, be hopeful and excited knowing that. Alexandre Dumas was born into a world of poverty and raised without an education. He decided as a teenager that he was not happy with the plate that the world had served him, and he was the only one who could do anything about it. So, he created his own opportunities and taught himself to write. After years of struggle, he was finally recognized as an amazing author and cherished playwright. He is quoted as saying, "All human wisdom is summed up in two words - wait and hope"

Creating your own opportunities doesn't have to be this awe inspiring adventure. It was right after the darkness overtook my soul that my mother recommended a book to me. In the book that author repeated a quote that inspired her to follow her dreams. She had always wanted to be a writer even though the world thought differently. The book read "if you want to be a writer, you have to write, so write." This is when I became inspired to pursue modeling with every fiber of my being. I decided that if I wanted to model, I had to model, so I started modeling. There was no debate or a Pro's and Con's list that I wrote down, deciding if this was right for me or a good move. I knew that this was what I wanted and I was going to find opportunities to pursue my dreams at all costs. As long as the job did not compromise my integrity, I was going to take it. I saw a sign near my house that advertised an upcoming show, so I went for it, and I got it! I got an agent and I thought that she was in charge of finding me jobs, so I waited and waited for work that never came. That was when I decided that I could not leave my career in my agent's hands only, so I started searching for my own work. I started creating my own go-sees, I started reaching out to anyone and everyone that I possibly could, and it worked! I got booked for print ads and was direct booked for all kinds of shows. The next thing I knew, I was on photo shoots in Mexico and walking runways in Hong Kong. Things were happening for me, because I was making them happen. I came to a point where I wasn't satisfied with "good enough" and I knew that I wanted more. For me, that meant that I was going international. I woke up one April morning and made the decision, I was going to move to Taiwan and give it a shot. By May I was on a plane creating another opportunity for myself. When I got there, it wasn't all lollipops and roses. It was hard. It sucked pounding on doors and begging for work, but I grew so much from that experience, as a model and as a person. I constantly reminded myself that it's not personal. It is business, it is another opportunity. Eventually I was cast on a Taiwanese sitcom, and that is where my acting career began. One little moment out of millions changed my entire outlook, again. So often we take for granted those little moments that make such a difference in our lives. I don't look back at that adventure and remember all of the rejection or the hard times, I look back and I remember the little moments just like that one. You can create a million opportunities for yourself and you might only get one little moment of satisfaction, but it will be worth it. Eventually those moments will turn into hours of memories that will last a lifetime. Carpe Diem, my friends.

"Although beauty may be in the eye of the beholder, the feeling of being beautiful exists solely in the mind of the beheld." MARTHA BECK

CHAPTER TWO | BEAUTIFUL

IN MY OPINION, THERE ARE SO MANY THINGS THAT MAKE A WOMAN BEAUTIFUL. I do not believe that there is one preconceived type of beauty. Now, that doesn't mean that the people you meet at a casting don't have a lot of preconceived ideas in their heads. But that is not your fault. As long as you take care of your body and respect it the way that it deserves to be respected, then you will eventually be perceived in the way that you want to be, and by the people who matter. Yes, cheese fries are delicious. Yes, I can smell the donuts in the bakery when I walk by and the sprinkles sometimes dance off of the top of them spelling out my name and singing a show tune about their deliciousness.

But I have a goal. I have goals. And I cannot accomplish those specific goals if I am not properly nourishing my body. That all starts with not only eating less, but eating less of specific things, like sugar and high fat carbs (which turn right back in to sugar—might as well have had those two donuts and skipped the fries, huh?) Now I know that everyone needs a relaxing drink every now and then, but finding different things to relax you instead of alcohol is a big way to change your habits. Your body converts alcohol, especially when consumed in excess quantities above your normal diet, into sugar and stores the excess sugar. Reducing sugars doesn't just mean that you quit eating skittles every day after lunch. That includes your venti nonfat quad shot triple iced mocha lattes with whip and extra drizzle. That includes margaritas and daiquiris, even the virgin kind. Remind yourself that this is your LIFE. This isn't a diet or a way to lose weight. This is a lifestyle, a religion, it is who you are.

Slowly start to incorporate more protein in your diet. You don't have to start buying a side of beef every six months, devouring a steak at every meal. There are great proteins in all sorts of yummy stuff from beans to nuts and different vegetables. Boost up your intake of fruits and veggies and figure out ways to eat them differently so that you don't get bored with the food. It is really that simple. There is no amazing diet or trick to healthy eating. Eat proteins, fruits and veggies, and do so in appropriate quantities. Most restaurants don't serve "appropriate quantities." When you do go out to eat, just eat about ½ of what you are served, and that is most likely the caloric amount of what your body needs for that meal. Take the other half home and eat it when you are hungry again. I'm not telling you that you can't have a sweetened coffee or bahama mama every now and then, but it's all about moderation. Trial and error is really the best way to go about it. Everyone's bodies are different, so figure out what foods bloat you and what foods fill you up better. I love bagels, but I can tell you right now, there is no way I'm eating any bagels anytime near an audition, unless it is for a maternity ad. I'm like a blowfish within thirty minutes. I also have a big sweet tooth - I love dessert. And it is OK to have it - but a small bite/taste not an entire jumbo helping of double chocolate fudge cake with raspberry drizzle. (Okay two bites but that's it.)

Watch out for the sneaky stuff. Yes a salad is healthy. No a salad with fried chicken, ranch dressing, cheese, bacon and 700 croutons is not healthy. Grilled chicken salad, vinaigrette and a load of veggies is optimal. NO it doesn't taste as great, but it definitely feels better to your body, and feeling healthy will make you feel better on the outside. I have two specific rules that I want you to memorize.

1. *"Eat less, move more."*
2. *"If you are full- stop eating."*

Okay so you are eating healthy, and now your body wants some action. Being an active person is all about finding out what works for you, just like the foods you eat. I, personally, love the Insanity routine. It is all plyometrics (jumping) and cardio. There are no weights, no machines, no equipment to mess with. I have a friend who despises cardio. She loves Yoga and that works for her body type. You might not like cardio or yoga. Try swimming. There are so many ways to exercise nowadays that don't even feel like a workout (until the next day). Rock climbing gyms are sprouting up all over the United States and can provide people with a fun way to get some excitement and work out all at the same time. Simply walk places. Ride your bike. Help the environment and yourself simultaneously. Have someone who will tear you apart if you stop at the deli for a pastrami sandwich after you air up the tires on your Schwinn. Just commit and go for it.

Set goals with your food and your workout just the same as you do everything else, and hold yourself accountable. Find a buddy to compare results with and hold each other accountable. The list goes on and on. There is no room in your world for excuses so just give them up now. If you want this, if you want to be the healthiest, best possible, beautiful you, then you have to commit. Everything in life is about commitment. If you set attainable goals for yourself and commit to them, then the world is in the palm of your hands. It is so easy and straight-forward.

BEING BEAUTIFUL STARTS WITH A D.R.E.A.M.

1. DISCIPLINE. Make a chart. Be accountable for yourself. Everyone wants to earn

a gold star. The best of the best always start with a plan. Discipline is the key to succeeding in creating a Beautiful you.

2. RELAX.
Stress accounts for 75% of that bloated belly that you are trying to avoid. Breathing through your nose, taking ten minutes away from a stressful situation, exercise and meditation are all great tricks to relaxing. Take a tip from the Brits and drink a cup of herbal tea. Chill out, man!

3. EAT YOUR HAND.
Doctors say that every person's typical portion size should be about the same as the palm of their hand. If you can't pick up your serving of mashed potatoes with one hand then you've got too much.

4. AVOID PROCESSED FOODS.
If it grows or used to breathe then it is better for you than anything that comes out of a can or plastic bag, and usually cheaper. The more natural food that you eat in moderation, the healthier your body, skin, hair and mind will be.

5. MAKE OUT.
Kissing, hugging, loving, living. Have great relationships and let good friends in. YOU CANNOT DO THIS ALONE. If you are in a committed relationship, then you should practice *"loving"* ALOT. Sex is one of the best calorie burners and stress relievers readily available. If you are not in a committed relationship, stick to Yoga. Instead of watching that episode of Friends where Ross and Rachel kiss for the first time for the thousandth time, slap on your heels and take the stairs, practice walking in every possible situation until it is like breathing. Involuntary.

Okay so you are trying to push yourself into a world of spectacular things and one spectacular thing that is always present in that world is the extra-curricular activities that are sometimes mandatory. Learn to party without partying. Socialize without socially drinking. Be noticed without abusing your body. It is possible to do all of this- if you are committed. If you go out with a so-so attitude towards it, you are probably going to get sucked in by some crazy party girl screaming

"SHOTS!" across the room. You are going to be hungover and miserable within 24 hours and you will wake three days later with no chance to live those days over again. They are gone and you are asking yourself was it worth three hours of partying to give up three days that you could have spent creating your dreams? Probably not. Leave your house committed to your goals and go home proud of your self-control.

Finally, in this world of 5'11 beauty queens and Real Housewives with triple D's and inflated lips, learn to accept yourself for who you are. When you look in the mirror, remember that each freckle, crooked nose, bony finger and tall forehead was put there for a reason, and that reason was to make YOU more beautiful. Instead of trying to change who you are, embrace it. Exaggerate the things that you might think are flaws and use those things to make you unique. Take care of the body that you were given, and put you first. Invest in you. Of course grooming is important and bathing will definitely help with your acceptance at auditions and casting agencies. Don't tan and in the famous words of Kurt Vonnegut, wear sunscreen. Use lotion daily and be sure that you take the time to lube up every nook and cranny of that magnificent skin that you are wearing. It makes a difference.

Learn to relax. Stress makes you look older and angrier by the minute. Figure out what you need to do to relax. Whether it is meditation, reading, walking, hiking or some other inspirational activity, do something that is very relaxing to you at least once a week. I love massages and spas. You can get massages at massage schools for much cheaper than paying a professional so there is no excuse for you not figuring out a way to calm down, take a deep breath, and de-stress. It will be advantageous to you in the long run. Being the healthiest you that you can possibly be will create that external beauty that you are trying to portray. A person who is unhealthy and ugly on the inside will never be as beautiful on the outside as they could have been if they were healthy and beautiful on the inside. Whoa, that's a mouthful.

Get out a pen and paper and write down a quote that inspires you. It can be a line from a book or poem, a verse from a song, something a parent told you, or one that you have made up yourself. Tape it near a mirror that you look at yourself in every day.

Read that quote every day to remind yourself of who you are and that you are setting your eyes upon a beauty that is as boundless as that of the Mona Lisa.

You see, for years there has been no definition of beauty because the definition exists differently in every person's mind. There is no way that you will live up to the standard of what beauty is to another person. There is no way that you could even know or understand what that is because it is undefinable. You just have to accept that you are the epitome of beauty in your own minds eye, and once you do that, you will create a light that drenches the world and draws in every firefly that notices it. You will be irresistible, as long as you believe that you are irresistible. It wasn't until my 20's that I fully understood this. All my life I wanted so badly to fit in. I was taller and thinner and ethnically mixed. It felt strange to be so unique. But now, I wouldn't change any of it for the world. Even though I still get ridiculed for being tall and thin, I wouldn't want me any differently. I wouldn't know how to shop for clothing other than for someone tall and lean. I wouldn't know any other set of shoes than the ones with personality that speak to me. I am healthy and I love me. Every once in a while your reflection may become blurred by another person's negativity, but take yourself back to that quote that is taped on the side of your mirror and remember that there is no way that a person could tell you that you are not beautiful, because they don't even know what beautiful truly means. You are the only one who knows the definition.

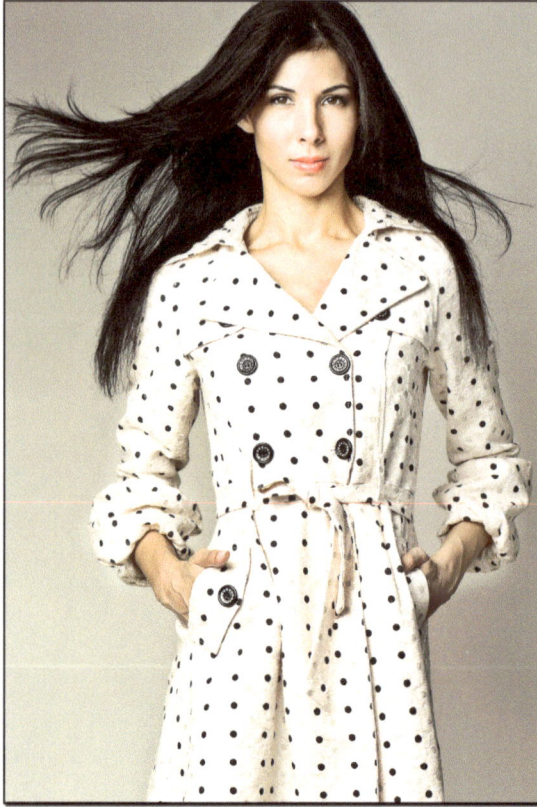

"*Fame is indeed beautiful and benign and gentle and satisfying, but happiness is something at once tender and brilliant beyond all things.*" MARY MACLANE

CHAPTER THREE | BRILLIANT

SO OFTEN WE HEAR THE WORD BRILLIANT ASSOCIATED WITH MANY DIFFERENT THINGS. It can be said about Albert Einstein or in reference to a stunning diamond. A devious plan could be considered to be brilliant by some people. Overall, the word brilliant has many different meanings.

BRILLIANT: {BRIL-YUHNT}

1. Full of light; shining.

2. Relating to or being a hue that has a combination of high lightness and strong saturation.

3. Sharp and clear in tone.

4. Glorious; magnificent: the brilliant court life at Versailles.

5. Superb; wonderful: The soloist gave a brilliant performance.
6. Marked by unusual and impressive intellectual acuteness: a brilliant mind; a brilliant solu-
tion to the problem.

Now that you see how much encompasses such a simple word, becoming brilliant is exciting, isn't it? It is such an amazing thing to have enough confidence that you can call yourself brilliant. To some, brilliance may seem unattainable, while someone else reading this is just now coming to the realization that they are brilliant, inside and out. So what can you do to increase your brilliance, shine up and glisten for the world? Education is vital. Whether you are gaining a formal education or you are educating yourself in an unconventional way, you are creating a better you, which is what being brilliant is all about. I have a business degree. I spent two years at a community college and five at a university struggling through work, my dreams, and life to achieve a degree that I believe will one day push me to the point where I want to be in the modeling world. After a year of exams that have an extensive fail rate, two years of work experience and lots of hurdles, I finally received that all important piece of paper that allows me to put the letters CPA at the end of my name. It's a nice accessory, let me tell you. But my point is that it wasn't easy. Achieving your dreams isn't always a walk in the park and achieving brilliance comes from lots of hard work and even more heart.

There are lots of unconventional ways to be educated without getting an "education." When I was on a photo shoot in Cabo once, I had to learn to paddle board in about five minutes. (Seriously? Hang on while I morph into Aqua-woman) Water freaks me out a little because I am not a strong swimmer, and I was not stoked to jump into the massive ocean on this tiny little board. While I was assured that it was safe and that this would be just like surfing (which I had never done before) I was still really uneasy about it. So, I put on my game face and I learned. I left knowing how to do something that I didn't know before. I left that shoot educated.

I don't dance at most of my photo shoots, but I take dance classes. I also take acting classes on a regular basis. Both of these things have proven to be helpful to me on various occasions. This is where you put your Bold, Beautiful, Brilliant plan into works. Whether you have to make a presentation to the stuffiest, most intimidating group of executives or are preparing for an even more devastating audience in a classroom full of High School Students, remembering that you are exactly where you want to be in your life, or at least on your way there, is all you need to come across as the confident, self-assured amazing woman that you are. If you have ever said to yourself, "Hey, I wish I could do that!" Go do it! Learn, try, fail, and succeed. Whatever happens, you will at least be able to say that you did it. My mother waited until very late in life to take art classes that she'd never had time for in the past. Don't wait, do it now, become brilliant. Become a sponge. Remember every single person that you meet and learn from them. People are placed in your path specifically for that reason. If someone tells you a story of their own success, use it to your advantage. Ask more questions than you might want to, and you will get more answers! The whole point is that you need to keep your brain learning in order to stay fresh and relevant. If you ever get to a point in your life where you feel like you know how to do everything that you could possibly want to do, then you need to look further and find something more. Never be satisfied, stay hungry! Life has so much to offer us that we never take advantage of. Learning new things will provide you with new experiences, and that will make you a better entertainer; a super-you! Enjoy your life! You only get one chance at today. "Sunshine creates happiness, and I create myself. Nights are long and life is predominantly good. Wind is refreshing. Tea is wisdom. Do the best you can, and be good to yourself so that you can above all be good to others." ~Jessi Lane Adams

A brilliant mind will know when things aren't right. You will be quick and sharp. If something sounds too good to be true, then it probably is. A brilliant person is not going to be desperate enough to jump into something that feels fishy. Do not go just because you want work. Do not go because you think there is a teeny tiny chance it is not too good to be true. Ask for references, ask for referrals and make sure that there is no possible way that this person is pulling the wool over your eyes. Stay brilliant.

Remember earlier when I told you about how I took off to Taiwan without looking back? It was an amazing experience for me that made me a more brilliant person.

I tried new things, explored a new culture and came home a wiser, more educated, ready to take on the rest of the world kind of person. I got on an airplane headed to a part of the world I knew nothing about. When I'd made my decision, I had to look up on a map where the island was truly located. I knew no more Mandarin than hello and thank you. I didn't have a place to live or a sole to lean on. I landed on soil that eventually stole my breath. I learned what it took to survive, what it took to live and what it took to be an amazing me. Knowing what I know now, I made a few mistakes and did many things the hard way. Without knowing the language, I am now very good at charades but I think that only adds to my repertoire of skills.

As an actress, I need to convey a message not only through words but also through gestures and body language. Those are things you can't learn in a classroom. Those are things you learn from living life. Putting myself out and reaching for those as like-minded as me, I met some amazing people and etched beautiful eternal memories in the back of my mind's eye. Looking back, it was a pretty silly thing to jump into so quickly, but had I the time to think it through I'm sure I would have thought myself out of it. And that would have been a mistake. Now, I'm not saying everyone should do the same. I love to travel and explore new places. By my mid 20's I'd lived in 4 different countries and likely will live in more. But what I am saying is to find your passion and don't be afraid to learn what it takes to be there and enjoy it.

Being Brilliant is also a culmination of being Bold and Beautiful. Once things start falling in to place, you don't have to try so hard to remember who you are and it just starts pouring out of you. One weekend, I was planning a HUGE editorial *(ended up being 14 unique looks)* and it was the first time I was in full control of such a huge project. I was creative director, coordinator, producer, visionary and of course cast myself as model. In the process, I had a photographer cancel, a hair person cancel and the week before the designer cancelled. Are you kidding me? Right then I should have lost it. But I don't let it get to me anymore. I am a trained machine that is ready for anything, and problems like this just help me to kick it into high gear. I had to implement my Plan B, Plan C and all the way to Plan *"OH SHIT"* and in the end, I think it was one of the best shoots I've ever been a part of. Things tried to stop me.

People didn't think I could do it. But I created this opportunity. I contacted the magazine editor to pitch my idea. I coordinated props and the team. I contacted many designers (of which most said no or no response) but it only takes that one who says yes. It is through perseverance and my own blood, sweat and tears that I made this opportunity for myself. And it will be published in at least one magazine. I intend to submit it to the larger magazines too, but no one handed this to me. Sometimes I look in the mirror and I can't even believe that I did it. No one told me how to do it, I just figured it out. I do get a lot of people who ask me how I've done it. How do you get a body like that? How do you get the contacts/jobs/ experiences? But I don't have that answer for you. All I know is that I stay committed to being Bold, Beautiful and Brilliant and I don't let anyone or anything get in my way. I just work hard and go after it. There's no easier answer. I don't think I could recount exactly what it took to make things work that weekend.

"*Your greatest weakness lies in giving up. The most certain way to succeed is always to try just one more timE.*" **THOMAS EDISON**

MORE BOLD | MORE BEAUTIFUL | MOST BRILLIANT

A WELL-KNOWN SPEAKER STARTED OFF HIS SEMINAR HOLDING UP A $20.00 BILL. In the room of 200, he asked, "Who would like this 20 BILL?" Hands started going up. He said, "I am going to give this 20 to one of you but first, let me do this." He proceeded to crumple up the $20 dollar bill. He then asked, "Who still wants it...?" Still the hands were up in the air. "Well," he replied, "What if I do this?" And he dropped it on the ground and started to grind it into the floor with his shoe. He picked it up, now crumpled and dirty. "Now, who still wants it?" Still the hands went into the air. "My friends, we have all learned a very valuable lesson. No matter what I did to the money, you still wanted it because it did not decrease in value. It was still worth $20. Many times in our lives, we are dropped, crumpled, and ground into the dirt by the decisions we make and the circumstances that come our way. We may feel as though we are worthless. But no matter what has happened or what will happen, you will never lose your value. Dirty or clean, crumpled or finely creased, you are still priceless to those who DO LOVE you. The worth of our lives comes not in what we do or who we know, but by WHO WE ARE. You are special—Don't *EVER* forget it."

Living your life for today is an amazing free gift that people are given. It is also a gift that is rarely used. Procrastination is an easy way to give up before you've even started. The funny thing is that so many people think that getting started is the hardest part. I don't agree. Getting started is tough, you have to commit, you have to continue, but you should also never be satisfied. Aristotle said "We are what we repeatedly do. Excellence, therefore, is not an act, but a habit." Once you form those habits that make you Bold, Beautiful and Brilliant, keep striving for more. Learn more, travel more and go after things that you would never have dreamt of. Try not to ever get to the point where you say, "Okay, now all of my dreams have come true." Keep dreaming. It's easy to dream when things aren't exciting or when your world is a mess, but dreaming when everything is all that you could expect it to be is a habit that should be formed by every Bold, Beautiful, Brilliant woman.

If you have perfected the most difficult pose that the Yogi has to teach you, move on to lifting weights. When you are calm and organized at work but your mind is still dreaming, write a book, read a book, dream a story. There is no defined ending to what you can become and accomplish. Use the tools that have been outlined in this book as a skeleton to keep you together, but use the tools that you have been blessed with to be the heart, lungs and brain of a well-oiled machine that is out to conquer the world.

"Be yourself, fill your life with good people, and don't get a big head. It can all be gone tomorrow." MOLLY SIMS

ABOUT THE AUTHOR

Aubrey Rinehart is an accomplished model, actress, and talk show host with a passion for reaching out to other women. This step-by-step guide has an efficient formula that can be used to help women realize how BOLD, BEAUTIFUL & BRILLIANT they are from the inside out. From the aspiring model to the business savvy graduate who is trying to find her place in the world, Aubrey has inspiring words of wisdom that will teach you to believe in yourself in your darkest hour and like the phoenix, rise up and be all that you were created to be. This book is a must-have for the teenage girl that is trying to fit in and for the twenty-something that is trying to live up to world-defined standards. Full of tricks of the trade, real-life stories, and inspiring thoughts, Bold, Beautiful, Brilliant will leave every woman with a heart full of confidence and a mind that is set on reaching her goals.

www.ingramcontent.com/pod-product-compliance
Lightning Source LLC
Chambersburg PA
CBHW041802040426
42448CB00001B/10